Dont Go Broke Trying To Be A Business Owner

7 Secrets every business owner should know before you go out of business!

By Taurea Avant
Tywauna Wilson
Nik Sallie Franklin, Esq.
Toni Moore
Foreword by Trevor Otts

Copyright © 2020 by Taurea Avant

All rights reserved. This book or any portion thereof may not be reproduced or used in any manner whatsoever without the express written permission of the publisher except for the use of brief quotations in a book review.

Printed in the United States of America

First Printing, 2020

ISBN: 9798677320408

Edited & Formatted by Show Your Success

Published by Taurea Avant

Dedication

I want to dedicate this book to my number one fan. The woman who continuously speaks life into me. The woman who no matter what I do and don't do, loves me unconditionally. You are my biggest cheerleader... My Mom Veronica Terry. I love you!

Table of Contents

Acknowledgments vii

Foreword xi

Introduction xv

Chapter 1: Know your worth 1

Chapter 2: Let's Talk About Leadership! 11

Chapter 3: Sales Success Funnel 21

Chapter 4: Brand Development 31

Chapter 5: Poor Financial Management 41

Chapter 6: You Must Protect Your Brand 49

Chapter 7: Entrepreneurship Ain't for Everyone 59

Conclusion 77

Business Listings 79

Acknowledgments

I wanted to especially thank those people who supported this book before it was even printed. You guys and your faith in the information that I bring means a ton to me and I appreciate you all tremendously.

Laura Jones
Shachena
Phylisa Dever
Javis Taylor
Angela Amazin Tate
Cassandra Mouton
Tori Hollingsworth
Tammie Martin
Norma Mclauchlin
Karen Brown
Constance Neal
Kristin Douglas
Tolya Bennett
Jassminn Parker
Brian Olds
Stephanie Smith
Joyce Rogers
Lisa Boyd
Lola Ayers
Sonja Keeve

Acknowledgments

Rhonda R Bundy
Arica Quinn
Herin Bolivar
Andrea Shadd
Sakeisha Hylick
Janet Fowler
Chantay Bridges
Jacquelyn Heard
Edeline Francois
Joy Gage
Calandra France
Isabel Rojas
Lindsey Vertner
Mercy Myles-jenkins
Leticia Ay
Kr Henderson
Lisa Bailey
Wanda Hollis
Darling Moore
Carol Craven
Randall Minniefield
Rue Mayweather
Tikila Adolph
Carlette Whitlock
Bryan Willis
Tywauna Wilson
Corey Milton
Felicha Jones

Acknowledgments

Deshonda Jennings

Ida Hood

Yusheeka Gray

Lynda Goodwyn

Sydneykelliee Driver

Ashley Williams

Monique Somerville

Teasha Jenea Ross

Adrienne Burgess Boose

Queashar Halliburtron

Kandie Martin

Lashan Gunnels

Tishike Pennington

Chanel Spencer

Lashan Gunnels

Raymond Baxter

Bridgette Carter

Mone't Long

Teia Acker

Foreword

Brought to you by Trevor Otts

www.Instagram.com/trevorotts
www.BlackCEO.com

There is today's business owner, today's modern business owner, and then there is every other business owner. But today's modern business owner is willing to embrace the role of the disrupter. This book is for the disrupter in you. This book is designed to disrupt you because every business owner is a disruptive force for change in the world. And so what is disruption? Disruption is challenging the norm. As business owners, we have to challenge what our clients normally think, what they normally say and what they normally do.

As thriving business owners, we also must be willing to challenge what we normally think, what we normally say and what we normally do as business owners. We must be willing to challenge what the industry normally thinks, what the industry normally says, and what the industry normally does because we have to be willing to embrace the role of the disruptor. This book, these experts, these gurus, are here to disrupt the way that you have ordinarily done things.

They say that the definition of insanity is doing the same thing over and over again and expecting a different result. Well, let me introduce you to Insanity 2.0. That is doing the same thing as everybody else and expecting a different result. So as you turn each page of this book, understand that you have a responsibility. A responsibility to not just be a difference-maker but to be different. Today is the day when you embrace your role as a disruptor.

And so take out your pens, take out your markers and be ready to embrace the change that is now your destiny. This is the beginning of a movement, a disruptive movement, and every movement must have a moment. Those moments must be disruptive and disruptive moments within your movement that give it momentum.

Foreword

Remember your brand, your business, even who you are as a person were never created to be the same as everyone else. You were created to be original. If two of us are the same, one of us is not needed.

Today is about you stepping into your original, your original purpose, your original plan, your originality. So as you read this book, be the original because you were created to be that.

Introduction

First of all, congratulations on grabbing a copy of this book. This is by far one of my most favorite books that I've ever completed, and not just because it's the latest, but it is one of the books that I'm telling you from experience. I've been an entrepreneur since 1999, and ever since I could imagine, I've always wanted to be able to own my own business.

However, through trial and error, I've learned a lot along the way in the first 10 years of business.

I was very unsuccessful when it came to business, and that was because I was lacking so many of the things that are talked about in this book. I've also brought in some of my expert friends that can give you some additional tips in their area of expertise.

Now, if I were to give you any instruction or any tips on using this book to your best advantage, I would first say make sure you read it through from beginning to end, then make sure that you also go back and highlight the areas that connect to you most.

Be sure to go and download some of the bonus goodies that are available to you by simply going to bonus.nobrokebusinessbook.com. Hit me up on social media and let me know your thoughts.

Introduction

I really hope that you enjoyed this book as much as I enjoyed putting it together. I can't wait to hear about your success!

Let's get started.

CHAPTER ONE

Know your worth

Know your worth

I promise you this: If you truly understand the worth that you offer when it comes to your product or your service, this is going to take you to the next level. It's not about having thousands and thousands of followers. It's not about getting on every single news platform. It's not about speaking on stages over and over and over. Because the truth is, you could get all that exposure, but if you don't know the specific worth that you offer, guess what's going to happen? There will be no money in the bank. Nobody's going to pay you. You must know your worth and your purpose.

And I want you guys to understand when I say worth, I'm not talking about in general terms. The value that you bring. Like SPECIFICALLY what is it that you do and offer? When people say, I help people to find their deeper desires within their heart or I help people to understand their purpose, that is not specific enough. Now, before you get an attitude with me (lol), I want to ask you a question. How many people who teach others how to know their purpose and worth, and are truly building a six and seven figure business?

I'm not talking about influencers and/or celebrities. I'm talking about a person who you never heard of who uses that as their RESULTS. If that is you and you can prove it to me, I will give you a FULL refund of this book. I promise it. Matter of fact, you don't even have to prove it. Just hit me up. I got you!

Now if you are hearing other people say that and it's not working for them, why on earth would you follow that same tactic? You've got to dig down deeper. Why does someone want to know their purpose? What is knowing your purpose going to do for you? Is it going to increase your income? Have better relationships? Are you going to be happier? You truly must understand that. So, let's dig into this chapter and I hope you enjoy.

If you are having trouble with identifying your worth and purpose, be sure to get access to my bonus training that I'm sure will help you. Go to bonus.nobrokebusinessbook.com

The Generalist Syndrome

In this particular chapter, you're going to learn a lot. But most importantly, my goal is that you're really able to hone in on understanding who it is that you are.

So, the first thing we have to talk about is many entrepreneurs having what I like to call the generalist syndrome. You've probably heard the quote, "Jack of all trades, master of none." Well, honestly, that is what takes place in the world of entrepreneurship today. I see so many people trying to be the expert in everything that they know how to do. They end up confusing their entire audience that they have been able to capture.

It is so important that you don't want to get into that phase of trying to be the end all and be all for every single thing that you know how to do.

I believe that you should figure out the one thing that you are good at and that you love doing. You don't have to try to do everything just because you have a little bit of information or experience in that. Become a specialist. Become known for that ONE thing. The truth is, when you become a specialist, people will pay you more money.

If you can relate to what I'm saying, it's important that you want to get out of this whole thing of trying to do all and be all. Please, for the sake of your success, figure out the one space, the one result that you can become known for.

For example, John C. Maxwell is known for leadership. If you haven't heard about him, check him out. He has written several books on leadership. He has sold millions of books on leadership. And he continually comes out with new books on leadership. That is his base. This is his NICHE. Now, it's not to say that that is not the only thing that he teaches or that he sells. But he is known for leadership.

And that's what you want to do.

Who do you serve?

It's important that once you have figured out the one thing that you want to be known for, you need to know who you serve.

I have been coaching thousands of people and the number one thing I hear all the time is "I help ANYONE."

If you're trying to help everyone, you're honestly helping no one. Think about it like this: The challenges that a 15-year-old has are totally different than the challenges of a 25-year-old, which are totally different than the challenges of a 40-year-old. The challenges that a married woman has are totally different than the challenges of a single man over 35. It is important to narrow down your audience.

I understand that it's scary to hone in on one specific type person that you serve because you feel like you'll lose a lot of money. But the truth is that many entrepreneur don't niche down their audience, which means their audience doesn't know that they serve them. You've got to figure out that specific person. And the one thing that I would recommend is look at yourself. What are some of the characteristics about you? And then you want to go after those particular people.

What results do you deliver?

Ok let's keep this train moving. By now you're understanding that it's time to become a specialist in ONE space. You must also know the results. Time after time after time, I sit down with speakers and coaches that want to take their business to six figures. I sit down with aspiring entrepreneurs who want to be able to build a six and seven figure empire, but they have no idea about the results they offer.

For example, let's say that you sell makeup. Many people think that the results that they sell or the results that they offer are makeup. But that is not the truth as a makeup artist or selling makeup. As a makeup artist, You sell confidence to an extent. You help people to feel beautiful or enhance their beauty. Let's say that you want to get more specific. Go back to the previous sub chapters where we identify who we serve and how we specialize in that.

As a makeup artist who has their own product line, what would you say is the reason people should buy from you? Maybe you decide that you want to target women in business who really don't know much about makeup but they're extremely busy. And you want to create a line that will allow them to be able to get their makeup done, utilizing simple techniques in a short period of time. You could literally make a whole entire movement behind helping women in business to make their face up fast.

Unfortunately, a lot of makeup artists and sellers try to cater to everyone, and this is their mistake.

I don't know about you, but I really don't like a whole lot of glitter on my face. This is my own personal preference. I don't want to wear glitter on my lips, and I don't want to wear glitter on my eyes.

And so, when somebody promotes something with glitter, immediately I'm turned off because as a busy businesswoman that's not really what I personally like to wear. Another thing I don't like doing is spending a lot of time trying to put together makeup. In fact, I hate having to wear makeup if I don't have to. But I know that sometimes you've got to spruce up your face for a broadcast or an event.

I would love if somebody came out with a line specifically taught, targeted or tailored for women in business who don't have a lot of time or don't like to spend a lot of time on their makeup. I need an easy gliding eyeliner. I need perfect lipstick with lipliner, along with perfect foundation that covers everything without needing concealer. I would love for this to be in all ONE package.

So again, my question is, do you know the specific results that you offer? What is keeping you from going to the next level?

Turn it into Multiple Streams of Income

Now that you have figured out who you serve and how you serve them, it is so easy to turn this into multiple streams of income. Now, I do have another chapter where I talk about understanding the difference between multiple streams versus multiple businesses. So, I won't get into full detail here. But what I will tell you is that just because you only sell one product does not mean you cannot turn that into a massive empire.

For example, let's say you sell scrapbooks. How can you turn scrapbooks into multiple streams of income? Well, why do people buy scrapbooks? They don't buy scrapbooks just only to "scrap." Maybe there's a feeling that they get from doing scrapbooking. So that's ultimately what you sell when it comes to scrapbooking. You're not necessarily selling the scrap book yourself. You're selling the feeling that people have when they make them.

And so now you can create your own line of books. You create a course. You can have your own glue. You can have your own scissors. You can even have your own T-shirts. You can create a conference on scrapbooking. You could do quarterly events. There are so many different things that you could turn that one product into to create multiple streams of income. And this is where you really want to be.

We'll talk more about multiple streams in a later chapter. But I hope you have had a big AH-HA moment. In fact, if you have, please be sure to let me know. Go to bonus.nobrokebusinessbook.com join the private group and be sure to let me know if you've had a break through.

Chapter Two

Let's Talk About Leadership!

This chapter is brought to you by Tywauna Wilson

Tywauna Wilson
www.trendyelitellc.com
www.Instagram.com/Coachteewilson
www.facebook.com/coachteewilson
www.linkedin.com/in/tywaunawilson

Let's Talk About Leadership!

Tywauna Wilson is a best-selling author, entrepreneur, medical laboratory scientist, and an award-winning leadership maven. She is the Owner/Chief Leadership Consultant of Trendy Elite Coaching and Consulting. She is the Visionary Author of the "Leadership Tidbits" book series and host of the "Leadership Tidbits with Coach Tee Wilson" and "eLABorate Topics" podcasts. Tywauna has over 15 years of laboratory leadership experience. Her mission is to empower and train one million leaders worldwide to be able to utilize their skills to lead with confidence and leave a career legacy that makes them proud.

A message from Tywauna

When it comes to building leadership skills, I want to help entrepreneurs up level their strengths and have the skills that it is required to be an in-demand leader that stands out, get seen, and get rewarded in their businesses and communities. I want entrepreneurs to invest in themselves and the growth of their businesses through reading books, mentoring, coaching, and training programs to develop a millionaire mindset like that of notable successful CEO leaders.

When you read this chapter, you are going to learn some valuable information and if you like BONUSES, I do have a gift for you. Simply go to bonus.nobrokebusinessbook.com to gain access to additional resources to help you grow as a leader in your business.

Leadership is VITAL

Leadership is so important. It's really critical for your success to survive and thrive in this rapidly changing environment. To be able to compete in a global economy, you really need to have leadership skills. Having leader skills will benefit you both personally and professionally and will enhance the way you think, communicate, and build relationships in your business.

When I talk about leadership skills, you might think of these as basic skills that everyone has. FALSE!! Not everybody has them. It's like common sense... it really isn't all that common is it? So, when I think of core skills that every leader needs to have to succeed in business as well as in their personal lives and careers, I first think about having active listening skills. You have to be able to listen to what your customers want. Listen to what your stakeholders need. Don't just listen to respond, but really listen so that you understand, so that you're able to hear them tell you what they need.

If you're able to do that, then they will give you the answers to solve the problems. And that will benefit your business. You will just need to implement. You have to have the ability to ask great questions. Leaders ask great questions. If you ask the right questions, you will be able to save yourself time and money in your business. What business owner couldn't use more time and money? Asking great questions allows you to negotiate better contracts and deals. It helps you secure better pricing. It also allows you to be able to price your services accordingly by asking the right questions so that you can move more product. This results in more money in the bank, Cha-ching!

As a leader, you must be able to delegate. Leaders know how to look at the big picture, delegate some of the non-revenue generating tasks so that they can focus on adding to the bottom line in their business. Don't try to do it all. You must have the ability to be able to coach and train others to help your business run efficiently. At some point, your business is going to scale and you're not going to be able to do it all on your own. You will need to be able to communicate that. Develop leader skills now and you will be prepared later.

Leaders are action takers and not afraid to accept responsibility. In business, you will have to be able to accept responsibility for things that are your fault and those that are not your fault. There are going to be customers that are not happy with your service or product. And you will need to be able to accept responsibility for both positive and negative decisions. You will need to understand the viewpoint of your customer so that you can move forward without providing a poor customer experience. As business owners, let your customers know that you appreciate them. Finally, you have to be able to have self and situational awareness so that you are able to recognize when things are out of alignment within yourself, in your business, and in the economy so that you can respond accordingly without getting overwhelmed or having increased anxiety.

Having Leadership skills is a non-negotiable if you want to be able to have a sustainable business.

How to Develop Your Leadership Skills

Great news! You can start to develop your leadership skills right away. There are many no-cost options and even more options that yields BIG results if you invest a little cash.

I have a few strategies to get you started. I'll start with some of the strategies that are no cost. Leaders are Readers! Most successful CEOs read 60 books a year! While you may not have time to read that many, you can start by reading a business book each month. This will allow you to stay current with relevant business trends. This book you are reading is a great start. There are also books on audio that you can listen to on the go. Super convenient. Listening to podcasts is another no cost solution. Whatever you want to know, there's a podcast about the topic. You can also use social media. There are niche specific experts on social media platforms from LinkedIn to Facebook where you can find help to develop your leadership.

One other option is to find a mentor. What does mentorship do for you as a business leader? It shortens your learning curve on grasping new concepts and it gives you access to increased business opportunities. Your business mentor can share their expertise and leverage their influence to get you into rooms that you may not ordinarily be invited or able to get in to. Having a mentor is necessary for your success. Please note that mentorship can be free or come at a fee relationship.

When it comes to paid ways that you can gain leadership skills, they can include webinars, virtual summits, niche specific or business-related meetings, and workshops. These events can range from a 30-minute presentation to a full day event in both live and virtual environments. Another paid strategy is to invest in a coach. No matter your business, you NEED a coach. Coaches help guide you to reach an agreed upon goal typically over a specified period through specific steps. A coaching relationship is a partnership — coaches help you change your behavior and achieve defined solutions. If you need accountability accomplishing your Leadership goals and want to see results quickly, coaching is the way to go!

Do all business owners need leadership?

Absolutely. If you want to stay in business and not spend unnecessary money, you absolutely need leadership. Leadership is influence. Leadership builds trust. You need to be able to communicate and connect with your target market if you plan to get sales and generate revenue. Everyone communicates, but leaders know how to connect with their audience and sell to them based on their behavior. You develop this insight by using your leadership skills and gaining trust.

Leadership matters in service and product-based businesses. You must practice active listening so that you can hear the voice of your customer. When you're dealing with people, when you actively listen, they will tell you everything that you need to know. They tell you the types of products. They make you aware of any issues they may have with your service quality as well. When you are in tune with their wants, you can quickly respond to issues in the event they arise without getting overwhelmed. It is bound to happen at some point in your business that someone is not going to be happy about your product and/or service. How you respond could be the difference in your business being sustainable or not. It takes a lifetime to build a credible brand. And it only takes a few minutes to tear one apart.

Again, leadership affects everything. It affects you as a person, your purse, professional brand, and your business. If you want to create a sustainable business, you must continuously learn, develop, and sharpen your leadership skills. Get so good with your leadership, that people will want to work with you because they know the value that you offer them. Be able to answer the "why" questions, which is extremely important in your business. Why your business? Why your service? Why your product? Why your service? Why you?

Leadership has its benefits especially when you take the time to develop it. If you have any doubt, research Microsoft, Inc. and its leader.

Mistakes business owners make

I find when it comes to mistakes, business owners don't stay intentional about investing in their leadership and personal growth. Instead, they get distracted with trying to learn how to do everything in their business. And what I mean by that is, as business owners, we are trying to learn everything all at one time, and when we do this, our focus gets split on trying to do everything but what we should be doing. This starts to take the attention away from the product or service that you offer. By continuously investing in your leadership, it allows you to continue getting good at your craft. Continue to hone down on that.

I also find that business owners don't take the time to get comfortable with public speaking and their presentations skills. Get comfortable preparing and delivering presentations that resonate with your audience so that they begin to know, like, trust, and want to buy from you. This will not only add significant value to you as a person but also to your business.

Another mistake is not being able to outsource and allocate activity. This has to do with your ability to manage projects, delegate accordingly, and follow up. Be aware of your weaknesses or your areas in which you have opportunities to grow. If that includes outsourcing your accounting or bookkeeping because you're not good at that, you need to recognize where you have limitations. Proper allocation of tasks is going to save you time and money alone. Again, it's so important that we don't get into the trap of trying to do it all, which results in an average but not exceptional business. And no business owner wants to be average.

Oh, one more thing – don't get shiny object syndrome. I'm guilty of that. Don't find yourself investing in too many tools that you get distracted. Instead of all different tools that you "feel" can help your business, be sure to invest in your professional development and leadership skills. Get laser focused and figure out what your strengths are and how those play out in your business. Evaluate your limitations to see where you need to outsource or get training. After all, that is what leadership is all about! Surround yourself with a support team and have systems in place that allow you to operate in your strengths. For your business, this means more money. Cha-Ching!

CHAPTER THREE
Sales Success Funnel

Now, this is probably my favorite chapter because this is where you're going to learn about how to turn your business into a strong foundation. It's all about building a success funnel that's going to allow you to build up your clients and build a strong foundation, along with having time and freedom. I don't care what product or service it is that you sell. Every single one of you can build a powerful success funnel that will keep you in a position where you're not running around like a chicken with your head cut off.

In this section we will figure out how to turn what it is that you've been called to do into a success funnel for details.

Multiple streams VS Multiple Businesses

I see people get this confused all the time when it comes to building their business. Many people think that multiple streams are the same thing as building multiple businesses. Now, let me give you an example of what I mean by multiple businesses.

I had someone come to me and they had started a company where they were helping and coaching individuals to achieve a specific result. They started this coaching business. And they gave people the specific result. Then they were on Facebook and somebody shared some information about a home-based business. They joined and then tried to start to promote that business too. Their audience started to get confused and they lost clients.

Now, if anybody knows me, you know that I have been in two network marketing companies where I was able to make over six figures in each one of those companies.

That industry blessed me and taught me a lot. However, one thing I will tell you is that you cannot build a six figure network marketing business trying to do other businesses at the same time. It takes complete dedication, all day.

When you are trying to start up different businesses that have nothing to do with each other, they all require your time to be successful. This is what happens to a lot of entrepreneurs today. This is going back to the generalist syndrome. It's also some generational things that have to do with this. I won't get into that in this book but it has a lot to do with how were taught how to make money. You've got to pick one area of expertise and learn how to turn that into multiple streams of income.

Now, when I say multiple streams, let's go back to the initial one thing they (my client) wanted to coach in. They wanted to give a specific result. Now, let's say that they would have focused in and honed in on that, and as a coach, you can build multiple streams of income. You could do one-on-one sessions. You could do quarterly bootcamps or quarterly private group sessions. Then you have your coaching program. Those are three different streams of income.

Then could sell a t-shirt. That's another stream of income. You could also create a book. Of course, you know, I recommend you have a book. Every entrepreneur should have a book. You also could have a journal. I'd literally just named more than five streams of income. And what you do is you learn how to individually promote them. Just because it's one business does not mean that one business cannot turn into multiple streams.

But here's another exciting thing. Even in that space, you can still generate more streams of income. You see, there's no additional work that you have to do when you're in, other than making the connection. This is why it's so important to understand there's a big difference. So, you can still focus on your coaching business and at the same time bring in additional streams of income.

Hook Item

When it comes to business, one thing people love is free things. And it's a way to connect with others and give people an opportunity to connect or get to know that person they're doing business with. Another thing that I've come to learn is that when people do business with you, it's because they know like and trust you. And so, creating an opportunity to connect with them with a hook item is something that is very essential.

Now, the hook item is going to be a free product or service that you're going to give away to people so that they can get a taste of what it is that you do or sell. When I was in the network marketing industry, both companies had a hook item. One, we used to sell these girdles where you could put the girdle on and immediately you would get an hourglass shape.

That hook item was putting a woman in one of those sample girdles and allowing her to see the results that she wanted to achieve. Now, granted, many women, as soon as you put that thing on them, they did not want to take it off. They were ready to pay full price for it. It was one of the most ingenious businesses I had ever seen because literally all we had to do was convince you to let us put you in this garment and you were going to buy it.

The results of this hook item was them getting that experience. I was then in a coffee business where our hook item was giving people a free cup of coffee. We would show them how easy it was to make the coffee. All they had to do was get hot water and pour the mixture into the hot water. And then they had a fresh brewed cup of incredibly tasting coffee. See, I want you to understand that in any product-based business, there's a way that you could hook individuals.

Now, maybe you can't afford to give somebody something for free, but you could give them a special discount. You see this a lot of times people say, hey, join our list and get 20 percent off your first order, 30 percent off your first order. Now, if I were you, if you really want to separate yourself and you're in a space where you're selling a product, make it so that at least on the first product that they buy they get a really nice discount.

I could be the first product only that you break even with – don't let yourself lose money but give them a substantial discount. Not one of these little 10 percent discount, but something that's going to make them fall in love. Because then once they get the product or the service, they're going to love it and want more.

When I got into the coaching space, my hook item consisted of so many different things from doing a free webinar to a free workshop to even a free e-book. When it comes to coaches and speakers, hook items are easy to create because you can just create something like a simple e-book that's just a few pages long that gives value. I also have another hook item where it is a free master class where I teach people how to write a book.

But this should get you started.

Intro Item

So for everyone reading this book, I always recommend your Intro item be something that's lower priced and really easy to purchase. I believe every business owner should write a book because that book is also a way that gets you additional exposure. People see authors as the expert. And when you are the expert, they will buy. Let me give you another example. Let's say that you have a clothing store and you figured that your target audience is going to be single women, helping them to get cute, beautiful dresses that make them stand out and look real fly.

So, you target single women. Well, you can create a book about styles or clothes that can make you irresistible to your future or current man. Now you have a book that positions you to get on the media and you're talking about what your expertise is in. And guess what they're going to want to do? They need the clothes. So, they're going to buy your clothes.

I always recommend offering an entire intro item, but it can differ depending upon who you are or what your product or service is.

Core Item

Your core item is going to be that next level up. And this may be priced between $97 to $197. Now, for some of you, if you've been in your space for a little bit longer, it's going to be priced more. I know some people whose core items or middle item might cost an investment of $997 to $1997 or even more than that.

It just really depends on what your final product is. So you want to figure out what's going to be that middle-priced item. For me, my middle item is my 3 Day Boot Camp or my Platinum Book Writing Program. This is where we help our clients to get their books done. So for you, what would be your core item? In fact, I would love to know. Let me know by visiting my Web site. Bonus. NoBrokBusinessBook.com and you'll get a chance to post what yours is! You might even win a gift from me. I love doing giveaways!

Premium Item

Your premium item is going to be your higher ticket item. This is the ultimate goal. The ultimate produce or service that you offer. This is the end in mind. This is where you really want to try to get people to buy your product. And please believe it does not mean that it ultimately has to be the last time that one particular customer or client purchases your premium item.

Many people who have their own online stores create some kind of a premium program that can allow people to get multiple products for one investment. You could offer multiple sessions. It could be a six-month or twelve-month supply or program. I would highly recommend figuring out what that could be for you. This makes things so much easier when it comes to building a sustainable and expandable business. So, what is your premium item going to be?

Many people take advantage of my premium once they have gone through my core program and had some success. But it's not something that I offer to any and everyone.

CHAPTER FOUR

Brand Development

This chapter is brought to you by Nik Sallie Franklin, Esq.

www.niksallie.com
www.Instagram.com/niksallie
www.facebook.com/groups/NikSallieHolisticHustle
www.linkedin.com/in/nicolesfranklin

Brand Development

Nik has over 18 years of experience in marketing and branding, having worked for Virgin records as a marketing rep in Dallas Fort Worth to support artists like Janet Jackson, Coldplay, Korn and Lenny Kravitz. She has over a decade experience in law specializing in intellectual property, specifically trademarks. Nik has also worked at Facebook for almost a decade, first in Intellectual Property Operations and now in sales in the Global Business Group, advising Fortune 500 healthcare companies on their advertising strategy. On average, she manages and generates 8 figures per quarter in advertising revenue. Additionally, she owns NikSallie.com, a trademark Law Firm supporting six figure women entrepreneurs in building and protecting their businesses so they can manifest their purpose into profits. Nik is also a Master Reiki Healer and was named a 2020 Woman to Watch by *Austin Woman Magazine*.

I work with entrepreneurs who have been in business at least two years. Their main challenge is not knowing how to communicate a cohesive brand that really speaks to their ideal audience and helps that audience convert from fans to paying customers.

In other words, my client is struggling to create an authentic brand that really speaks to who they are and calls in the right people to their business. Once we finish with their new branding or their intentional rebranding, the result is one cohesive brand that's professional, and will also build the "know, like and trust factor" between them and their customers. The second thing that they're going to walk away with is a brand style guide, which is their "Brand Bible."

This resource ensures any business owner that their branding stays consistently professional. It's the foolproof guide for any vendor they hire because it's the official reference guide that houses all the fonts, colors, logos, and assets of the brand. This consistency leads to public recognition, which is the foundation for trust.

What is branding?

Branding the visual container that communicates the psychological and emotional imprint of a business, and the essence of its core values. Branding is responsible for how people feel when they interact with the business. At all times, it's a conversation amongst the company and its potential customers, customers, and non-customers.

You can also think of branding as the overall look and feel of a company in regards to the goods and services that it's offering.

Now when it comes to branding, there are specific elements that should be included. Think of the brand and the company as a literal "person." This "person" needs to be clear about their mission statement, core belief and ideal customer. And then from there, what's the best way to communicate with this ideal customer? The frequency? Through what channels, e.g. social media, email, etc.?

What's the nature and tone of those conversations? Will the brand voice be uplifting, witty, energetic, or calm and subdued?

Just like a person has a personality, so does the brand. So, the person who is building out this brand really needs to pay attention to who they're speaking to. And remember, you only get one time to make a great first impression. What impression do you want your brand to lead with?

How to market your brand

When it comes to marketing your brand, the number one mistake you want to avoid is trying to talk to everybody by considering everyone your potential customer. You must remember that you're not for everyone and everyone is not for you. And that's not a bad business mistake or a bad business mindset.

That's you putting up boundaries that will allow you to market to the right people in the right way, to those who want what you have to offer. It will also allow you to use your energy in the most efficient way as you decide how you want to set up the marketing. So really, when you set this intentional boundary, you're saving yourself time, money, and energy because now you're super focused on exactly who you need to be serving.

Now that you know who you're marketing to, you want to figure out the best channels to reach these people. Ideally, online channels, such as social media, will provide you the reach, scale, and personalization to speak to your audience effectively. So, it's best to focus your attention there.

When you use social media, you're going to use it organically, meaning you can post content for free. But beyond that, you can find interest groups online that cater to your ideal customer and offer to do a webinar or promotion that drives value for the audience, while providing you exposure.

In summary, when you market your brand, the very first thing you must do is know who you're speaking to and who you're not speaking to and be OK with that. And the next thing is figuring out the marketing channels through which you want to reach these people and know that you're going to post on your own. But then you can also leverage other people's presence and their audiences as well to reach the right people and provide additional value to them.

To social media or not

When you are looking at the power of social media and whether you want to try to leverage that, one of the first things you want to do is decide where your people are.

Have you done the research to figure out whether your ideal customer is on Pinterest or Instagram or some other platform? You don't want to spread yourself too thin by starting eight different social media accounts and then not having the time, energy or focus to keep them regularly updated. Not only will that cause you to spin your wheels, but it will also look unprofessional because your brand won't look cohesive, professional, or trustworthy.

Less is more when it comes to social media. If you can have two social media accounts that are well-managed and regularly updated, that will serve you much more than having eight social media accounts with low quality, directionless content. So, when you're looking at social media, decide which channels your people are on and focus on nurturing those channels.

The next thing to think through is whether you're going to leverage free organic social media or invest in paid advertising across social media. From a budget standpoint, I would recommend that you post organically first to build a following and raise awareness about your business. Then, once you get to a certain point where you have some revenue, you can then build out a marketing budget. The main thing you need to keep in mind with social media is consistency. Getting a content calendar together immediately will help you understand when, what and why you're posting content. Marketing is like dating – you'll need to take time to allow your audience to get to know you and build trust. Eventually, they'll be head over heels and swiping their credit card because they love your products and the value you provide.

So, to social media or not? Absolutely. Social media is a great tool to reach your ideal audience. Just be sure which social media channels you want to use and use them consistently.

For a free calendar template that you can use go to bonus.nobrokebusinessbook.com

First plan of action

The first plan of action when you are working in your brand is to have a solid business plan in place. I have met entrepreneurs in the past who have either not started a business plan or have not completed one. The business plan will form the foundation for your branding because it will lay out your competitors, ideal customer, pricing, and other considerations, including your marketing channels.

It's from there that you start to form your branding as far as your brand voice, because now you're clear on who you're speaking to. And no, you don't need a 20-page business plan. It can literally be a one-page business plan that includes all the main sections that you need to know. In fact, you can find a one-page template online by doing a simple Google search.

To gain access to a template that I've used, you can go to bonus.nobrokebusinessbook.com

After your business plan is complete, pull out the sections that describe your products or services, your pricing, and your target customer. And from those three sections, you can start to build out the core pieces of your brand. And the main thing that you want to have as a deliverable from that is your brand style guide.

Remember, your brand style guide is one of the best and easiest ways to keep your brand consistent, strong, and recognizable, no matter what vendor, partner, or organization you work with to promote your business. Also, remember to take a step back every now and then, take off your business hat, and step into the shoes of your ideal customer. How does your brand look and feel to you? What is it communicating? Would you be excited to buy your product or service? Take those insights and keep improving your brand, year after year.

Chapter Five

Poor Financial Management

Poor Financial Management

This chapter is all about financial management, and I'm going to be honest, financial management is not one of my favorite things to do. Honestly, I just love to be able to walk in my purpose and do the things that God has called me to do.

But when it comes to handling your finances, this is so important. It's vital that you do understand how your finances are working and that you are protecting yourself. And so, if you do learn one thing from this chapter is get you someone who is good in this space.

In fact, I probably mentioned my website over and over lol but go to bonus.nobrokebusinessbook.com, because I have some professionals that I can connect you with, but I'm speaking from experience.

If your finances are not in order, you could be putting yourself into a lot of trouble. If you're not having your records in order, you could be putting yourself into a lot of trouble.

If you plan on making good money, you got to make sure that your finances are in order.

I'm a true believer that God will not give you more than you can handle. And so, if you can't handle a little, it's difficult to handle a lot.

Take it from me – I have experienced challenges in financial management in all areas that this is something you do not want to skip. Get your stuff in order.

Set Goals

OK, so let's talk about setting goals, because I think this is particularly important. Many times, when I sit down with clients, the first thing that I like to ask them, especially when they're wanting to write a book to grow their business, is how much money do they want to make? The truth is that most people that I sit down with don't have a specific goal when it comes to their income. They are focused more on where it is that they want to be.

Many times, I've heard people say, "I just want to be successful," or "I just want financial freedom." But the truth is that if you don't have a specific number, then it's exceedingly difficult to get to something that's very general. So, you've got to be specific. The first tip that I can give you in regards to setting goals is how much money do you need to take care of your expenses?

I'm not just talking about your business expense, but also your living expense and living from not just only paying your rent and your bills, but also for the additional things that you want to do in your life.

I am not a big believer of working only to pay bills.

I believe that you should work to live life and so make sure that your goals do incorporate the things that you want out of life, the things that will make you move, the things that will excite you.

What to do with a dollar

In my book, *A 6 Figure Vision*, I break down what you should want to do with a dollar. The reason why this is so important is because many people that I come across, they're just making money and blowing it. In fact, if you're one of those people where you've made money and you're trying to figure out what did you buy with your money, then you want to understand what to do with a dollar.

In fact, if you would like a free copy of my book, a six figure vision just go to bonus.nobrokebusinessbook.com. You can get an entire book for free and you'll be able to get the chapter where I talk about what to do with your dollar.

But let me give you a summary of what I talk about in the book.

When it comes to understanding the income that you have coming in, you also need to identify the income that goes out, keeping in mind that you have your personal expenses, your living expenses, your business expenses and even your taxes. You want to make sure that you are allocating money and setting it aside so that you're able to live a successful and fulfilling life.

So, don't just go spend all of your income only on your business or all of your income only on yourself.

Make sure that you have allocated your money so that you are not in a position where you're stressed out and trying to make a dollar stretch because money, it doesn't stretch.

Taxes will get you

So let me tell you something about taxes, if it's one thing I have come to learn is that is something that you cannot avoid, especially if you want to be able to make sure that you're running your business legit and legally..

Many times I find that business owners especially that come from where I come from do not do their taxes right and go to these "free" services companies instead of having someone who is a specialist who can help you in this area. Trust me… if you plan to make big money, you need a specialist in the tax area. Im not talking from what I've heard, I'm talking from what Iv'e experienced.

For me, this is not my expertise, and this is not something I love to do when it comes to handling my taxes.

This is why I have someone on my staff that can help me with this.

In fact, I have someone who helps me with my balances every single month. And then I also have my tax preparer who makes sure that all my stuff is correct. One thing I can tell you is what you never want to do is get in trouble with the IRS. They can garnish your wages, and they can revoke your traveling from traveling abroad. They can do so much. They can take away a lot of stuff from you.

So, make sure you do not skip out on this. Make sure you do not avoid this.

Too many of us are failing in business because we're not taking care of our taxes.

If you would like to access some of my tax professionals who have helped save me from hundreds and thousands of dollars in tax relief, make sure you go to bonus.nobrokebusinessbook.com.

Trust me, I've got the best of the best and they will make sure that you are straight.

Insurances needed

Having insurance is also something that is especially important. Now, again, I'm not an expert in this space, and so I will make sure that if you go to bonus.nobrokebusinessbook.com, I will connect you with some incredible insurance agents.

There are all types of insurance that are available to you as a business owner. I'm not just talking about car insurance or health insurance, but insurances that are designed to protect you and your assets.

You want to make sure that when you are running a business, especially if you're working with clients and customers, which all of us should be, that you are protected on all ends.

Also, there are special insurances in case something is to happen to you and you're not able to earn a living that you're still able to take care of yourself. Guys, the unexpected can always happen. The worst thing you would ever want to do is build up a business that's earning you a significant income and God forbid something happens, and you're now not able to earn an income. Get insurance before it's too late and you make sure to properly insure yourself so that you can continue to keep running your business.

Chapter Six

You Must Protect Your Brand

By Toni Moore

www.tonimooreesq.com
www.Instagram.com/Tonimooreesq.com
www.facebook.com/tonimooreesq
www. linkedin.com/tonimooreesq

You Must Protect Your Brand

Toni Moore, Esquire is an Intellectual Property Lawyer and Bankable Business strategist with over 20 years of experience. Throughout her career, Toni has been helping authors, speakers and creatives transform into powerful and profitable CEOs in business.

My legal firm is committed to helping our creative clients appreciate that their intellectual property is their most valuable business asset. And we help our clients capitalize on their intellectual property by building, branding, and banking their brilliance. The first thing we do is legalize their business so that can separate themselves from their business brand. In doing so, they limit their liability in business. Second, we help our clients protect their brands through intellectual property registration, licensing, and policing. For bonuses on trademarking and even tax information be sure to act by going to bonus.nobrokebusinessbook.com and I'll be sure to be in touch with you.

When to Trademark

The best time to trademark your business name, product and or services is when you don't want anyone to capitalize on the creative name of your product, program, or service. Without a trademark registration, anyone can duplicate what you do. When I'm asked when the best time to trademark is, I ask the person whether they are committed to the brand so much so that they would have an emotional response if someone else used and monetized it in business. Without an emotional response, there will be no financial commitment.

Take me for example – Legally Chic is one of my brands. I did not have Legally Chic 22 years ago. Also, to be honest Legally Chic is probably the fourth time around for me to work in business for myself as a lawyer. So sometimes if you're a creative person, you can go through so many different brand names. But when you know within your soul that you want to be the sole producer of the brand, then you trademark it.

So, if you happen to fall upon that exceptional brand name in the beginning, then it's always best to register as soon as you can. Just know anyone who uses the branding during your indecision, they have a common law interest in that branding just as much as you do. They can then turn around and register just as quickly as you. But at the same time, if you say, NO, I'm going to wait until I get bigger and make five hundred thousand dollars or wait to have a million followers, you could then lose the brand because it became generic.

Another consideration is that you can't cease and desist on any one if you have not first registered the brand as a federal trademark. If you don't have a registration, you cannot stop others from using your common law brand. Now if you are like I was and you are going back and forth of being not sure of your brand, I want you to fully appreciate what happens when you wait. Just know, the longer you wait, the more you allow other people to penetrate on your marketplace, your reputation, and your positioning. So, it's ultimately going to be a CEO decision whether this is right for you. It costs money to do good business.

If push came to shove, I would rather have you trademark the brand. If you determine later that the brand mark/log is not right for you, you can sell it to someone else or you can assign your rights to another person or company. You can also license your trademark to other people as opposed to you allowing anybody to capitalize on your intellectual property.

Mistakes made when trademarking

One of the big trademark mistakes is that business owner's mark is registered in the wrong international class. Typically this happens when you try to trademark on your own. Or, some of these online services that help you to do it for less but don't consult you on who, what, and why. Many times, you will end up spending more because you have a higher chance of doing it all wrong.

An example of trademarking in the wrong class could be that you have a T-shirt that you sell through your coaching business. Or maybe you give T-shirts to your coaching clients. You think, I'm going to trademark my name as a

T-shirt. Well, you just trademark your name as a T-shirt, but really your money maker is coaching, speaking, selling, having conferences, trainings, and certifications.

You definitely want to trademark in the area that you don't want a competitor to come and get a derivative. Many people think that "I have a trademark, I have a registration, and nobody can use it because its trademarked." If you use the wrong class, then you are wrong. You did not trademark the business services. You did not trademark the business conference. So, you are not protected if someone goes in and starts using your brand name in the area that you monetize.

Another mistake is that they do not trademark quick enough. As I said before, the longer you wait, the higher your chances are that someone may start using your brand. Other people don't have to respect your brand and they can replicate your brand if you don't make it a priority to protect your brand with a federal trademark.

Another mistake is that business owners allow too many people to use their brand without an agreement. When there's no agreement as to who owns the trademark or anyone sets boundaries around it, you can also get into trouble. Just do a quick search on ex band mates who fight over the brand name when they break up. Similarly, nonprofits with chapters run into this problem too because when there is no boundary in place there is no way to create boundaries when there is a problem. And when you allow too many people to use your brand, it's becomes hard to identify the brand creator of the goods, products, and/or services.

The last mistake I wanted to share is that a trademark registration identifies the source creator of intellectual property. It's a digital asset. So, the question sometimes becomes, well, who owns it? Should the individual own it, or should the company own it?

Are you going to let the company own it? If you are operating your business in the nonprofit sector, I'm just letting you know right now that if you are the creator of the brand you should not allow your nonprofit to be the registered owner of the trademark. As a reminder, if a nonprofit closes its business, all the assets must be transferred over to another non-profit. Similarly, if you are running a for profit company such as a limited liability company and it goes out of business or the company must file for bankruptcy, your company may lose the rights to your trademark. Legally speaking, if you as the individual owner owns the registration, you may lose your right to the trademark registration if get married, divorced, or become insolvent. There are so many legal considerations regarding ownership, but I don't want to belabor the issue. Just know that under trademark rules, the owner is the decision maker.

To sue or not to sue

Keep in mind, litigation is always costlier than registration period. If another company is using a trademark, the question is how long were they using it? Remember if a person waits to register the brand, as I said before, anybody can use it. If there is no certificate, anybody can use it. But if you are the rightful owner of your trademark and you are the originator, you may have to consider whether you want to sue another person to stop them from monetizing your brand. Where state related violations, you may retain counsel to file a Cease and Desist Order. If someone filed a trademark registration, you may retain legal counsel to file a Petition for Cancellation. And if you have a registered mark and notice a new registrant trying to capitalize a similar mark, you can retain legal counsel to file a Petition of Opposition. We had a couple of litigation processes and I realized that the importance of a trademark is that once there is a certificate, you can confiscate any products or services that is violating your mark and monetizing your brand.

For example, have you heard of *Entrepreneur* magazine? *Entrepreneur* has registered several registrations to exclusively capitalize on the word, entrepreneur. Anybody who uses the word entrepreneur, they are always going to oppose it and they don't care how much it costs. Why? Because they know that their trademark, their brand is more valuable where they are the dominators in that area than allowing other people to water it down. Have you ever heard of Google? They are always in court responding when people try to say that their trademark is no longer a valid mark because it has become so generic. In response, Google persuades the court that they have differentiated themselves from other brand so much so that their brand is not a verb but the go-to resource to search the web.

Here is another example: Beyoncé's daughter Blue Ivy and Blue Ivy Catering have had legal challenges before. Blue Ivy Catering had registered their mark and later opposed Beyoncé's registration by saying that her registration would create market place confusion. The Opposition litigation became a long process wherein Blue Ivy Catering used tons of arguments to preclude Beyoncé from registering. But in the end, the courts agreed with Beyoncé and allowed her registration to go through. In brief, the court didn't think that the services Beyoncé intended to render would be so similar that the public would be confused by the two brands.

If you need to make sure you trademark your business the right way, be sure to reach out to me and get my bonus material. Go to bonus.nobrokebusinessbook.com

CHAPTER SEVEN

Entrepreneurship Ain't for Everyone

Entrepreneurship Ain't for Everyone

Entrepreneurship is not for everyone. That's one thing I've come to learn. Is that being an entrepreneur is not everybody's role in life, and it is OK. We live in a world where sometimes people will try to make you feel bad about working. In a career or working in a place of employment, but honestly, for me, I now tell people that that is a true blessing.

Some of us have been called here to do different things and show our strengths in different ways. Because listen, entrepreneurship is not easy. I always joke about it that you've got to be a little bit bipolar to be an entrepreneur because there's going to be days where it's up, days where it's down. There's going to be days where you're crying and days where you're laughing. There's going to be days where you got money coming in and days where you don't. I don't know why in the world anyone would want to be an entrepreneur.

In fact, I'll never forget graduating from college with my bachelor's in computer science ready to work an incredible career. That's what I thought was going to be my journey.

I had tried entrepreneurship so many times prior to then and just always tried and quit. Tried and quit.

I knew in my heart that I wanted to be one, but I didn't know if I really wanted to do this thing. Now, looking back, would I change anything that I've ever done? Absolutely not. But I promise you, there have been nights where I've been to my knees crying and weeping to God.

What's my next move? There have been days where I've questioned how am I going to pay the rent and survive another month?

There have been days where people have said certain things about me that have hurt me to my core, knowing that I'm ultimately trying to do my best to impact people, but I've had to learn that I'm not called to inspire and impact everyone.

Again, if you ask me would I change any of this, no, I would not. But I do want you to understand that this journey is not easy. And if you find that it's not for you, it is OK. It truly is! It's OK to be happy doing what you do. So, go ahead and enjoy this chapter.

Practice what you Preach

When it comes to truly building a business, I believe that if you're going to promote a product or a service, that you also must be a product of that product or service. Listen, nobody is going to believe in the results that you claim that you offer if you're not using it for yourself. Think about it.

If you go to a hair growth specialist and they don't have any hair, how many people are really going to believe that they can help them with growing their hair? Yes, they may have some before and after's, but the way that I think is that if you're not willing to use the product on yourself, then why would I use it for myself? You must make sure that you practice what you preach.

Another thing about me, because I'm in the coaching space, is I never tell people to do something that I don't do myself. For example, even in this book, you're going to see different people that I'm naming and thanking, different companies that I'm promoting. And the reason is because they supported me and preordering this book. This is one of the techniques that I teach to my clients on how to make money with your book before it comes out.

Everything that I teach my students to do, you better believe I practice it myself. It's nothing worse than having a coach, a speaker or a business owner tell you about a product that you know for sure they don't even use themselves. I be like chiiiilllle please, if they don't go somewhere with that, because I don't play those games.

Self-Motivation

I saw a post the other day from one of my coaches who was asking a question about motivation and many times I had people come to me and ask me how to get motivated. If it's one thing that I have continuously believed is that if you are a person who needs other people to motivate you, it'll be difficult to sustain motivation for a long period of time as an entrepreneur.

When it comes to being a business owner, you are responsible for your own time. The majority of the time, there is going to be nobody calling you up to see if you've done the work that you've promised to do. In fact, many days I don't talk to anyone at all.

I've had to learn that to be self-motivated. It wasn't my clients. It wasn't my team. It was all due to deciding to stay motivated. Now, granted, yes, there are many times where there are many of my clients who will share with me testimonials that inspires me and gets me excited. And yes, my team tells me how much they are grateful for me. Which, by the way, I am so grateful for anyone who has ever invested at least one dollar into anything that we do, because you have trusted me with the money that God has given to you.

Also, let me just say, anybody who has ever dedicated at least one-minute working and helping to continuously grow the movements that we have created over the years is such a huge blessing. But when it all boils down to it and when it's all said and done and you are sitting there looking in the mirror, nobody is going to drag you to success. I like to say this all the time. Stop waiting on people to save you. You have to do the work.

I hear people say this so recklessly. The saying that "faith without works is dead". The reason I say recklessly is because I don't know if people truly understand what they're saying.. Faith means doing it even when people laugh at you. Faith means doing it even when you have failed at it. Faith means that every single day that you step out here to do something that you've never done.

There's going to be challenges that come along the way and there are going to be times that you're going to feel like giving up.

But guess what? You've got to stay focused.

Sacrifices will be made

Now, I want to tread very lightly on this subchapter because I don't want you to think that you must give everything up in order to obtain success. There was a time when I was in the industry of network marketing where I made so many sacrifices that honestly, to this day I have not been able to bounce back from. I've lost a lot of relationships because I was so laser focused on being successful in these companies that I turned people off and I turned them away.

When I talk about sacrifices, I'm not saying to necessarily sacrifice people who are in your life that are not necessarily supposed to be connected to your business. Not everybody is going to be your customer and they're not supposed to be. But when I do talk about sacrifices, I talk about sacrificing time away from some of the things that you like to do..

Me, I love going to the movies. If I could go to the movies every single day, I probably would. However, in the process of trying to grow business, I realized that I probably can't go to the movies every single week.

I started making it a reward system. If I was able to accomplish something, that I could go to the movies.

Now, some of the most important sacrifices that every single one of you must be willing to make is to sacrifice your thinking.

The reason why we are not where we want to be has everything to do with the way that we think. Our thinking is truly what causes us to take the actions that we take. And sometimes our thinking can be affected by the people that we are around. So, you must sacrifice the thinking that you have always had and learn how to develop and evolve it.

Now, in the process of changing your thinking, yes, there may be some people that you identify that are not really supposed to be in your life anymore, but don't kick people out of your life just because they're not supportive of your business. The people that I'm talking about are the ones who when you are around continuously bring your energy down. The haters who never have nothing good to say. Anyone who is just not helping you on your journey to improvement. Even if its just having someone to let your hair down with. You still have to be careful with who you are around even in those times.

Also, I've learned who I can talk to about certain things when it comes to my life. You have to have the right conversations around the right people. Everyone aint ready for your self-improvement or business success.

As a business woman, there are just some times where I don't have business talk around my loved ones. I've had to learn to sacrifice, telling them about the successes that I've had, hoping that they'll see the excitement or be inspired to want to start a business. I just focus on talking to them about the things that family and loved ones talk about. These conversations typically are about family news or things like that. But, yes, there are going to be sacrifices made. And no, you're not going to be able to do everything that you want to do.

And my question to you is, are you willing to make those sacrifices?

Communicate Constantly

Communication is something that is very important. And to be quite honest, I am not a big phone person. I'm not a big talker... Well in certain environments lol.

I don't like talking on the phone for long periods of time. Unless it's my boo thang lol. I also don't like long emails from people. Communication for me is something that, as an introvert as well as a loner, has been something I've had to improve. However, what I've learned is that it's not just about communicating.

It's about being effective with your communicating. I believe the reason why I don't like talking on the phone for long periods of time is because I don't like to have conversations about anything other than something that is productive. Now, I'm not just talking about money, but I mean in life. I've grown to a point where I just don't like having meaningless conversations anymore. So, when you're bringing on team members, the great thing about that is that you're not having meaningless conversations.

I've learned how to be able to create systems within my company as well as schedules that can allow me to effectively communicate with the people that I have on my staff all at one time. So that way I'm not bogged down with talking to someone every single day about something that could have been handled on one group call. Also, you need to know how to talk to people when you're growing and expanding your business. You're going to have different personalities. And everybody's personality may or may not be like yours,.

More than likely, if you are an entrepreneur and you're running a business that has survived longer than two years, you probably have a strong personality. And the truth is, many of the people that come to work with you or for you are probably not going to have a strong personality. I have a strong personality, and have had to learn how to be effective with my communication. I've had to learn how to not be the bad girl or bad guy.

If you want people to stay with you for long term, you must know how to be effective in communicating to people. There are some books that I can recommend to you for this skill set. Just go to bonus.nobrokebusinessbook.com for the books.

Always Be Growing

Now, for those of you who are part of the grammar police already know that this is not the proper way to say it. Well lol by now you done caught a lot of off grammar. But if you've been following me for a long time, you also know that I like it.

Always be growing. I had to learn that if I was going to be known for helping speakers and coaches to grow their business, and if I was going to be known for truly helping people to create books that are building and generating multiple streams of income, I had to continuously grow in that space. I'm always taking courses on books and learning how to write books, even though I've been doing it now for years.

I'm always plugging into leadership training. I'm also always plugging into marketing training and different things that I can learn to be able to take to the people who have entrusted in me that I am the expert. I've learned that growth is something that never ends. You must continuously seek growth, especially if you plan to build an empire and leave a legacy. I'm always going to conferences. I'm always reading books.

I never want someone who is interested in me to teach them how to succeed to ever feel like they're catching up. No offense, but if I'm going to be your coach, you best know that I will continuously grow.

Think Creatively

Now, please do not skip over this chapter or at least the sub chapter, because I need you to start learning how to think outside the box. A lot of times people always say to me to how do you come up with all these ideas?

Well, the truth is, I'm not that special. I'm not that smart. But what I do is I make sure to continuously surround myself with people who are innovative thinkers, even if they're not in the same space that I'm in. They may do something totally different than what I do. But I like to be around people who continuously stretch me.

I also don't want to do the same exact thing that somebody else does. I was on somebody's training and they invited me to be one of the speakers. And as I was listening in to some of the other speakers, I heard someone that noticed that I was on and was teaching the same exact thing that I taught. And not only did they teach the same exact thing that I taught, but I could tell that they were taken a lot of the concepts that I've created over the years and trying to reteach it to that audience.

Now, this is where you need to make sure that you protect yourself legally, which I hope you guys to plugged into that chapter if you've not already done so.

However. That right there was silly to me because the people that follow me know that that is my content. And people started reaching out to me and telling me all about it. Guys, the last thing you ever want to be seen as someone that is stealing somebody else's property, whether it be intellectual or their physical property. Learn how to take something that someone else is doing and make it your own. Create your own sayings, design your own logo.

Separate yourself from the crowd. Don't just fall in line and regurgitate.

You've got to separate yourself.

Now, let me give you another example: Blockbuster. For those of you reading this book, maybe some of you don't know what Blockbuster is. Well, Blockbuster was an incredible movie rental company that you could go to and rent your movies.

We started getting into the digital age, where people were really doing more things online and wanted something a little bit more convenient. Well, this company came out with this product called Redbox, and you could actually just go to any grocery store or any kind of pharmacy and you'd see a Redbox outside where you could go up there and rent the movie. No person needed; no membership needed. And you get your movie.

And then if you were late, it wasn't a whole lot of money for late fees like you would get at Blockbuster.

But then there was another change: this company came out called Netflix. Netflix took the concept of what Redbox was doing, but now you no longer needed to go to a physical store location. You just simply needed to have a device that makes your TV what is called a smart TV. And you can watch as many movies as you desire.

See, they didn't create a blue box movie rental space. They took the concept of what Redbox was doing and made it better. This is why you very rarely will see a Redbox outside of any more stores, because now everything is digital. This is what thinking creatively can do for you.

Know when to give up

I am not about to be doing a business for years and years and years and seeing no results. That just absolutely makes no sense. Honestly, if you have been in your business now and it's been several months and you're not seeing the type of results, you have to ask yourself, is this possibly not the business for you?

I'm not saying that entrepreneurship may not be your thing, but maybe this particular business is not the one. How do I identify results? Well, identify results of by having clients or by having customers.

You also must evaluate, is this the proper business for you just because somebody else is doing this and having success? This may not be your calling.

I truly believe what the Bible says – that God will make room for your gift. But if you've been working and you've really been working on this business and it's not giving you the success you desire, the success that you need in order to sustain and or grow, then this may not be the right one for you.

Got to know when to give up. You've got to know when to take your losses and at the same time, don't just take it as a loss, but take it as learning lessons for me. I knew it was time for me to walk away from the industry of network marketing, no matter how crazy people thought I was, because I was walking away from an industry that had paid me multiple six figures a year.

Now, no matter how deranged they were telling everybody that I was I was I still walked away because for me, I knew that that industry was simply a stepping stone for what it is that God has called me to be. The same question is for you. And please know that sometimes giving up is not easy to do. You must be ready. You must be willing to know when to give up.

In it for the right reasons?

Another thing that we should understand is that many of us are driven by many different ways or reasons. We like to have nice things and some of us like to be able to travel and some of us want to be able to provide for our family. Well, when I say getting in business for the right reasons, I'm not talking about that. I'm talking about ultimately. Getting into a business where you know that this is a God-given calling, that when you see people that have bought your product or your service and they're getting the results, that it does something to you.

I see many people get into a business because they see their fellow sister or fellow brother that gets into it and have success. And ultimately, they say, you know, I'm going to do that business, too. But that calling may not be your calling. And the way that you know is if you're able to wake up every single day and not have an urge to want to move forward. Or maybe you need to get motivated.

If somebody needs to excite you about your business, then this may not be the calling for you. I know some people who want to get in business only for money. The truth is this, as I've stated before, God will make room for your gift. You're walking in that gift that he is giving you. He's going to provide for you financially. He's going to provide for you in a way that you're not going to have to worry.

And you don't have to stress over just wanting to make money.

I've been in businesses where it was all about the money because I was surrounding myself around people who told me that's what I'm supposed to desire. They told me that's what success looks like. You must have money. And as I was making money, just as fast as it was coming in, it was going out. I'll never forget the conversation that I had with this young lady. I was telling her how much money I was making a month, and I was telling her how disappointed I was in myself because I had nothing to show for it.

And she told me that's because you've never assigned your money. That's when it clicked for me. That's when I understood that it was time for me to walk away from that business, even though it paid me very handsomely because I was in it for the wrong reasons. See, when you're in a business for the right reasons, you will find joy in it. You will not be stressed out. You will not be burnt out.

You will not find yourself in a position where every single day you're waking up dreading to get on that phone call or dreading to go into that office. Now, just because you're in a business for the right reasons doesn't mean there's not going to be hiccups.

There are going to be challenges. There are going to be times where you may wonder, is what I'm supposed to do? But it's very far and few between. So, make sure that you find the businesses for you. Make sure that you find what it is that you've been called to do.

And if it's not, move on.

Conclusion

Congratulations, you've made it to the end of the book. That means that you must have liked a little something of what you've read.

I am grateful for that. I also hope that you have taken time to go and get your free goodies that are available to you for simply reading this book. Also, make sure that you reach out to my expert friends, as well as those individuals who have contributed their business details in this book. I can tell you all of these people are serious about the space that they're in.

And even if you want to hit them up to find out how you possibly could get into the business that they're doing, I'd highly recommend it.

This book has been one of my favorites, and I truly hope that you enjoyed it.

Also, take a picture of you with the book. Tag me on social media. @VisionAvant on social media. You never know. You might just win a gift from me. I love when people show their support by visually posting on social media. I find that we don't do that enough. But the more that you do that, you'll find that you'll have more people willing to do that for you.

Again, thank you and congratulations on making it to the end. I'll see you guys in my next book.

Business Listings

Here are some highly recommended business that you can connect with. They may even be businesses that you can partner with.

www.deshondajennings.com
DESHONDA JENNINGS

📷 DJItTakesAVillage
f DJItTakesAVillage
in DJItTakesAVillage

DeShonda Monique Jennings is a wife, mother, grandma, and author. She grew up in a small rural town of Kenbridge, VA. In July of 1996 she relocated to the Richmond VA area. She has a Bachelor's in Accounting with a Minor in Business Management and a Degree in Early Childhood Development. DeShonda owned and operated a successful Licensed home daycare in Chesterfield County for over 10 years. She currently serves as an advocate and mentor for children. She is a firm believer of "It Takes a Village" when it comes to our youth. Her mission is to help 20 women start a home daycare.

LyndaBeGoodEnterprise.com

LYNDA B. GOODWYN

📷 LyndaBeGoodEnterprise

🅕 LyndaBeGoodEnterprise

🅛 LyndaBeGoodEnterprise

Lynda B. GoodwynCreating kick-butt strategies is Lynda's superpower. If you are a "solopreneur" stuck and need help transforming ideas to reality; using strategy mind-mapping, Lynda can help get you Unstuck! She's a proven Strategy Builder, skilled Communicator, people Connector, and effortlessly shifts between Strategic Thinker & Operational action taker. With over 30 years of corporate leadership expertise, Lynda has successfully transitioned from a high-demand corporate environment to building her own multi-business platform -- LyndaBeGood ENTERPRISE, Neora & Atlanta Life Media Agency. She's a newly published author and is currently working on publishing guided affirmation journals for little black girls.

www.reintromyself.com

LAURAETTE JONES

LauraetteJones

TheLauraetteJones

Lauraette Jones is no stranger to the bounce back. She has built a successful empire with her online clothing boutique (Her Achilles Heels), online hair company (KrounKare), and her Non-profit organization dedicated to help both victims and survivors of domestic violence (Kroun2Kroun). Each of these companies were birthed out of a traumatic journey she personally endured in life. Each experience has ignited her to passionately assist others to rebuild and reshape their lives starting from the inside out! She found the secret formula that led her to reframing and restructuring her thoughts towards herself, which increased her self-awareness allowing new opportunities in rebuilding her self-esteem, and eventually leading to a happier life.

www.sharhalliburton.com

QUEASHAR LANAY HALLIBURTRON

📷 qdpublishing

f msjillofalltrades

in queasharhalliburton

While many neglect to follow their dreams due to setbacks like procrastination, fear and a lack of resources, she uses those very things as stepping-stones to her success. For Queashar L. Halliburton, CEO and founder of Queashar Detroit Publishing, LLC, her greatest success to date has come from living outside the box and operating in her God-given gifts and purpose. In addition to producing her fair share of personal literary works, she works diligently to provide tools, resources and motivation for new authors nationwide positioning them to tell their stories and excel in the marketplace.

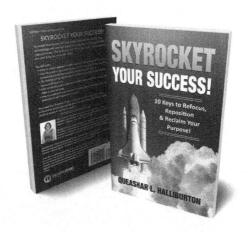

www.ruemayweather.com

RUE MAYWEATHER

📷 RueMayweather

📘 Rue.Mayweather

in Rue-Mayweather-jade61

Rue Mayweather is an International Bestselling Author. Rue is the author of two novels, No Gold At the End of the Rainbow followed by her second book in 2020 Recipe for a Man (She Thought) 12 Step Recipe To Finding Your King. Rue also is a collaborator on four Anthologies: Finding Joy In the Journey, How God Got Me Over the Curve During Covid19, Power of An Overcomer and Just Let Me Breathe. Rue has appeared on various talk shows in Dallas to include the Authors Lounge with Sheryl Grace and Whazup featuring military Sheros with Kim Wilson.

PHYLISA DEVER

📷 pmdbooks
📘 Phylisa Dever

I am a author and a entrepreneur. I own multiple companies. I had a incident to happen to me last year and it was devastating. So I wrote a book about it. It's called How To Properly Relate In The Ministry of Giving. It talks about how a Pastor gained our trust and then manipulated us to give him and the church millions. I also help people to not ignore or over ride your internal instincts. So that this will not happen to you.`

www.LegacyofLoveCoaching.com

LASHAN GUNNELS

lashangunnels

lashangunnels

We help people living with loss go through the grieving process, by helping them grow through the pain and step into their passion with and on purpose. LaShan is a mother of 8, grandmother of 18, and wife of an amazing husband for 20 years; therefore, she is passionate about helping people live their best life.

www.trendyelitellc.com

TYWAUNA WILSON

[O] coachteewilson

[f] coachteewilson

[in] tywaunawilson

Tywauna Wilson is a best-selling author, entrepreneur, medical laboratory scientist, and an award-winning leadership maven. She is the Owner/Chief Leadership Consultant of Trendy Elite Coaching and Consulting. She is the Visionary Author of the "Leadership Tidbits" book series and host of the "Leadership Tidbits with Coach Tee Wilson" and "eLABorate Topics" podcasts. Tywauna has over 15 years of laboratory leadership experience. Her mission is to empower and train one million leaders worldwide to be able to utilize their skills to lead with confidence and leave a career legacy that makes them proud.

wfiiservices.com
CONSTANCE MCKINSEY NEAL

◯ Wholefamilyinterventionservices

f WFISS

in mneal2

Constance Mckinsey Neal is a veteran educator from Louisiana who has worked with students' ages 0-18 for over 20 years. She is also involved in the mental health field providing psycho-education and counseling as a Mental Health Professional. She enjoys working with adults and children. She also enjoys spending time with family and friends.

www.re-definingself.com

STEPHANIE ROCHELLE SMITH

📷 stephanierochelleconsulting

f stephaniesmith

Stephanie Rochelle Smith, "From Loss to Self Love to Reinvention", is a shining example of what it truly means to deny yourself. One day while serving, she said to God, "Stretch Me". This wife, woman of God, mother, relationship expert and now best-selling author of "A Cracked Egg-A story of Loss and Love to Resilient Overcomer are the direct result of that one simple prayer request. Stephanie supports women who are Stuck, or struggling with trauma and loss, Reset the vision for their life and build Healthy Relationships. After Loss and Divorce, she embraced re-building herself and was determined to be an example to her daughter of how to win in life, love and business. September 2016, Stephanie married Alex and they are living out their fairytale and enjoying life together in Atlanta. Stephanie has been supporting women to rebuild the life they want since 2012.

Business Listings

www.kandieenterprises.com/
KANDIE MARTIN

- kandieenterprises
- kandieenterprises
- iamkandie

Kandie Enterprises, LLC is a media marketing company, we help small business owners to implement a schedule of consistency on social media. Which allows them to focus on their business while we focus on making sure they have a social media presence. What sets us apart from other companies is that we work with our clients to create their social media presence as well as take the worry of "did I post today" off of their shoulders. We also help them with making their websites, lead pages, logos and so much more.

Business Listings

DeShonda Jennings, Childcare Expert, DJ It Takes A Village LLC, @DJItTakesAVillage, www.ittakesavillage2.org

Carlette Whitlock (DaKiara), Publisher & Author, Mind Flow Publishing & Production LLC, www.mindflowpublishingproduction.com

Queashar L. Halliburton, Publisher, Queashar Detroit Publishing, LLC, @qdpublishing, www.sharhalliburton.com

LaShan Gunnels, Reconnection Life Coach, Legacy of Love Coaching by LaShan, @lashangunnels, www.legacyoflovecoaching.com

Constance Mckinsey Neal, Consultant, Mental Health Professional, Whole Family Intervention Services, @wholefamilyinterventionservices, wfiiservices.com

Rue Ja'Nelle Mayweather, Authorpreneur, Mayweather Books (Rare, Unique & Essential), @RueMayweather, www.ruemayweather.com

KR Henderson, Property Maintenance, Infinite Property Maintenance & Repair, @krnewvision,

Business Listings

Kandie Martin, Media Marketing Strategist, Kandie Enterprises, LLC, @KandieEnterprises, www.kandieenterprises.com

Lisa Stringer Bailey, Financial Professional, TripleM Money Management Matters, @managemoneymatters

Andrea Shadd, Spiritual and Business Coach, Spirit Life Coaching and Consulting, @Sunshine_Coach, www.spiritlif.org

Tywauna Wilson, Leadership Consultant/Executive Coach, Trendy Elite Coaching and Consulting, @CoachTeeWilson, www.trendyelitellc.com

Ida Hood, Health Coach & Certified Health Teacher, B U Fit,LLC, @idahood_, www.beautifullyyoufit.com

Arica Quinn, CEO & Author, Queen 2 Queen, @queen2queensvoice

Lynda B. Goodwyn, Strategy Specialist, LyndaBeGood ENTERPRISE, @lyndabegoodenterprise, www.lyndabegoodenterprise.com

Randall Minniefield, Brand Creator, YUNG MOGUL CLOTHING, @yungmogul_rann, www.yungmogulclothing.com

Business Listings

Mercy Myles-Jenkins, CEO/Founder, Legacy Driven Consulting & Publishing, @mercy.jenkins.1

DARLING MARIE MOORE, CEO, LIVING WITH DIVATUDE LLC, www.LivingWithDivatude.com

Joy Gage, Life & Motivation Coach, Canvas Coaching, @canvascoaching4real, www.thecanvascoach.com

Sakeisha Hylick, Relationship Expert, Marriage Can Win, @MarriageCanWIn, www.marriagescanwin.com

Brian J. Olds, Founder, Black Speakers Network, @BlackSpeakersNetwork, www.BlackSpeakersNetwork.com

Adrienne Burgess Boose, Legal Nurse Consultant/ CEO, Nu Visions Med Legal Consulting, @bosslady_legal, nuvisionsmlc.org,

Chantay Bridges, CEO, Bridges Publishing House, LLC,

Tishike Pennington, Founder & CEO, Divine Tees Co, @divineteesco, www.divineteesco.com

Monique G. Somerville, CEO, Monique G. Somerville Enterprises, LLC,

Business Listings

Dr. Lola H. Ayers, Pastor/Teacher, Kingdom Millionaire, @drlolaayers, www.lolalockettministries.com

Stephanie Rochelle Smith, Rebuild your Life after Divorce, Stephanie Rochelle Consulting, @Stephanierochelleconsulting, Re-definingself.com

Lindsey Vertner, Peak Potential Strategist & Speaker, Lindsey Vertner, LLC, @LindseyVertner, www.LiveAFirstClassLife.com

Calandra France, Credit Improvement Score Specialist, France Financial Services, @calandrafrance, www.francefinancial.net

Rhonda R. Hudgins, Owner, Metro Brag Bags, @RhondaRHudgins

SydneyKelliee Driver, CEO, Life Coach, Author, Speaker, Boss Up Your Life Academy, @SydneyKelliee, sydneykelliee.com

ShaChena Gibbs, Business Strategist, Real Sisters Rising Women Business Association, @realsistersrising, www.realsistersrising.com

Tammie M. Lilly, Tax Specialist, Why Your Refund Is So Low, @stagesofmylife

Business Listings

isabel Rojas'Lopez, Publisher, Rojas Publishing, @rojaspublishing, rojaspublishing.com

Angela Amazin Tate, Visionary Specialist Life Coaching, A Amazing Enterprise LLC. Coaching Services, @iamcoachamazin, Www.CoachAmazin.com

Yusheeka Gray, Personal & Business Credit Expert, DIY Credit Repair LLC, @therealcreditboss, www.diycreditclinic.com

Yusheeka Gray, Personal & Business Credit Expert, DIY Credit Repair LLC, @therealcreditboss, www.diycreditclinic.com

Norma McLauchlin, Publisher, Author, Coach, Chosen Pen Publishing, @chosenpenpublishing, chosenpen.com

Carol Craven, Cosmetics Line Owner, Lip-Candy.com, @caroldaniellecraven

Sonja A. Keeve, Podcasting Coach, Sistas with a Voice Podcast Network, @SonjaKeeve, Sistaswithavoicepodcastnetwork.com

Lauraette Jones, Motivational, Her Achilles Heels, @lauraettejones, www.haheels.com

Business Listings

Phylisa Dever, Entrepreneur, Kingdom Communications LLC, @PhylisaDever

Chanel Spencer, Maximum Evolution, @chanelspencernow, www.readytotransformnow.com

Bryan L. Willis, Sr., President, B-Strong International Athletics & Fitness, LLC a New Progress Ventures, LLC company, @theoriginalb_strong, b-strong.store

Made in the USA
Monee, IL
25 September 2020